Matter's Properties

by Jennie F. Crest

PEARSON
Scott
Foresman

DK

Describing Matter

Every living and nonliving thing is made of matter. Matter is anything that has mass and takes up space.

You can identify matter in many ways. You can use your senses to learn about the properties of matter. Look at an object to see its shape, size, and color. Some objects may feel smooth or rough. Some may feel soft or hard. You can identify some matter by taste or smell.

Performing simple tests on matter will show some of its other properties. See what matter does when you heat it or cool it. See how it is affected by a magnet. Find out if an object floats or sinks when it is put in water. Find out what happens when matter is mixed with other matter. Does any of the matter disappear? Is something new formed?

You can use a magnet to see what effect it has on matter.

States of Matter

Scientists know that all matter is made of tiny particles. These particles move. They are also arranged in different ways. The form, or state, of matter is determined by how the particles move and how they are arranged. Solid, liquid, and gas are the most common states.

Most things on Earth are naturally found in only one state of matter. Water is the only substance that is easy to find in all three states of matter. Liquid water is the same substance as ice, which is solid water. Liquid water is also the same as water vapor, which is water as a gas.

ice and liquid water

an ice sculpture

Solids

A solid is matter that has a fixed shape and takes up a specific amount of space. The particles are very close together. They move back and forth, but they are not able to slide past each other.

Think of a solid such as an ice cube. Its shape does not change. If the temperature is °0C or lower, the ice cube has the same shape in a glass or in a bowl.

Liquids

A liquid is matter that does not have a fixed shape but takes up a specific amount of space. The particles of a liquid are not as close together as they are in a solid. These particles can move and change places with each other.

Liquid water has the shape of whatever container it is in. It will take the shape of any glass you pour it into. If you pour it into a bowl, it will take the shape of the bowl. But the amount of water will still be the same.

pouring water

Gases

A gas is matter that has no fixed shape and does not take up a specific space. The particles of a gas are very far apart. They move in all directions. A gas always fills the container it is in.

Water vapor is a gas. Its shape and size changes all the time. Steam is not a gas. It is made of small drops of water.

steam

Measuring Matter

Balances, rulers, and graduated cylinders are some of the tools that can measure different properties of matter.

Mass

On Earth you weigh about six times as much as you would if you were on the Moon. This is because your weight depends on gravity. But your mass would be the same on Earth and on the Moon. Mass is a measure of the amount of matter in an object. Mass is important to scientists because it stays the same no matter what location an object is in.

A pan balance is one tool that measures mass. On one side of the pan balance, you can put an object that has a mass you know. Then you can put an object of an unknown mass on the other side. When the two pans are level, the masses are equal.

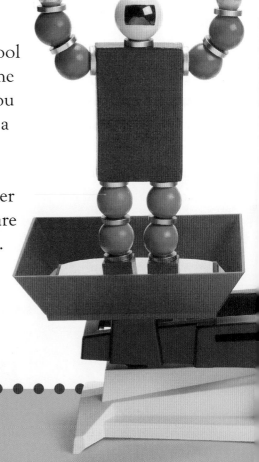

Look at the picture. The toy has a mass of 23 grams. You can take the toy apart and put the pieces on the other side of the balance. Both sides of the balance will be equal. The mass of all the parts is the same as the mass of the entire toy.

Mass changes only when matter is added or taken away. What if the toy were put back together in a way that looked different from the original toy? The mass would still be the same. This is because no matter was added or taken away.

Scientists use metric units to measure and compare matter. Mass is measured in milligrams (mg), grams (g), and kilograms (kg). The gram is the base unit of mass in the metric system.

The metric system is based on tens. The prefix at the beginning of the name tells what it is worth. One gram equals 1,000 milligrams and 1,000 grams equal 1 kilogram. A penny has a mass of 2.5 g. To have a mass of 1 kg, you would need 400 pennies.

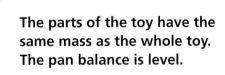

The parts of the toy have the same mass as the whole toy. The pan balance is level.

Volume

Think about blowing up a balloon. As the balloon fills with air, it gets bigger. The balloon gets bigger because the volume of air in it increases. Volume is the amount of space matter takes up.

Volume can be measured. A metric ruler can help you find the volume of a solid, such as a block of wood. First you measure the length, the width, and the height. Then you multiply all these measurements together. The block of wood may be 3 cm long, 4 cm wide, and 6 cm high. The volume is 3 cm × 4 cm × 6 cm, or 72 cubic centimeters.

Scientists use metric units to measure the volume of a solid, just as they do with mass. Some of the units scientists use are the cubic centimeter (cm^3) and the cubic meter (m^3).

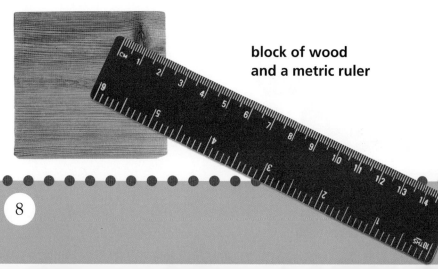

**block of wood
and a metric ruler**

The volume of liquids cannot be found by measuring length, width, and height. This is because liquids do not have a definite shape. You must use a measuring container, such as a graduated cylinder, to measure a liquid.

The volume of a liquid is measured in liters (L) and milliliters (mL). The units marked on graduated cylinders are milliliters. One liter equals 1,000 milliliters.

A graduated cylinder can also help find the measurement of a solid that sinks in water. First put some water in the cylinder and record the height of the water. Then add a solid, such as a ball. The height of the water will rise when you add the ball. The water level rises because the ball pushes away some of the water. The difference between the two water levels tells you the volume of the ball.

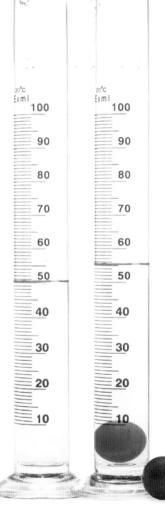

graduated cylinder

Density

Does tissue paper have more mass than construction paper? One way to answer this question is to get pieces of each kind of paper that are the same size. Then you can measure their mass on a balance. Another way to compare them is to find the density of each piece of paper. **Density** is the amount of mass in a certain volume of matter. If the tissue paper is the same size as the construction paper but the construction paper has more mass, then the construction paper has more density than the tissue paper.

You can find the density of an object when you divide the mass by the volume. Density is often measured in grams per cubic centimeter. Density is written as a fraction:

$$\frac{\text{mass in grams}}{\text{volume in cubic centimeters}} \quad \text{or} \quad \frac{\text{g}}{\text{cm}^3}$$

tissue paper

construction paper

cork — oil

plastic block — water

grape — corn syrup

Water has a density of 1. This is because 1 gram of water has a volume of 1 cubic centimeter. The density of an ice cube is a little less than 1. This small difference in densities means the ice cube floats in water. But since the difference is so small, most of the floating ice cube is below the surface.

The density of an object tells you whether it will sink or float in a liquid. Oil is less dense than water, so it floats on top of the water. The piece of cork is less dense than the oil, so it floats on top of the oil. The plastic block is more dense than the oil, but it is less dense than the water. So it sinks to the bottom of the oil but floats on top of the water. The grape is more dense than the oil and the water. It sinks to the bottom of the water. At the bottom is the syrup, which is more dense than all of the other objects.

Mixing Matter

A **mixture** is a blend of two or more substances. These substances can be solids, liquids, or gases. Substances in a mixture can be separated easily. They are not chemically combined. If you put together bran flakes, oats, and cornflakes, you would still be able to sort everything into separate piles. The bran flakes, oats, and cornflakes would taste the same whether they were separate or mixed together. All mixtures can be separated. Each part keeps the same properties it had before it was mixed.

bran flakes   oats   cornflakes

Most parts of a mixture can be easily separated. Suppose you put together sand and gravel. Would you be able to separate them? The sand and gravel are not joined together chemically, so you would be able to separate them. You could pour this mixture through a filter. This would remove the sand and leave behind the gravel. Both the sand and the gravel would still have the same properties they had before they were mixed.

This mixture is separated with a filter.

Solutions

Sugar and water can be mixed together to form a mixture. But you cannot see the sugar in this mixture. The sugar has broken down, or dissolved, into very tiny particles. The sugar and water have formed a kind of mixture called a solution. A **solution** is one or more substances dissolved in another substance.

mixing sugar and water

The most common kind of solution is a solid, such as sugar, dissolved in a liquid, such as water. In this solution, the sugar is the solute. A **solute** is the substance that is dissolved. The water in this solution is the solvent. A **solvent** is the substance that dissolves the other substance.

There are many solutions in the everyday world. Ocean water is a solution. Salt and other minerals dissolve in water. The air we breathe is a solution of different gases. The steel in buildings and cars is a solution. It is the result of a process that uses solids such as carbon and iron.

The sugar is dissolving in water, so the sugar is called the solute.

The ability of one substance to dissolve in another is its solubility. **Solubility** measures how much of a substance will dissolve in another substance. Sand has a solubility of zero in water since it does not dissolve in water.

It is possible to increase the solubility of a substance. One way to do this is to increase the temperature of the solvent. Cocoa powder will dissolve faster in hot water than it will in cold water.

Crushing a substance will also increase its solubility. A sugar cube will dissolve in a cup of water, but it may happen slowly. You can help the cube dissolve faster if you crush it into tiny crystals. It dissolves faster this way because more of the sugar is touching the water.

sand and water

Changes to Matter

Matter can go through both physical and chemical changes.

Physical Changes

Think about tearing a piece of paper. Doing this only changes the size and shape of the paper. The particles that make up the paper do not change. Any change in the size, shape, or state of matter is a **physical change.** The particles that make up matter stay the same in a physical change. But the arrangement of these particles may be different.

Is mixing sugar and water a physical change? In this solution, the particles are too small to see. But if you evaporate the water, the sugar will be left. The particles of the sugar and the water do not change, and they can be separated. So the mixing of sugar and water is a physical change.

Crumpling up or tearing paper is a physical change.

What kind of change takes place when a baseball bat is made? A piece of wood is cut and shaped until it looks like a baseball bat. The bat is still made of the same particles as the piece of wood. No new materials were formed. It has gone through a physical change.

Breaking a glass is another physical change. The glass is made of the same particles when it is in many pieces as it is when it is one piece. No materials are added or taken away. It only changes physically.

What if you dropped an egg, or cut up a potato? Are these physical changes? A broken egg still has the same properties that it had before it was broken. The potato also has the same properties that it had before it was cut. They just have a different shape than they did before. Both the egg and the potato have undergone physical changes.

Phase Changes

Water can be heated to form water vapor. Water can also be frozen to form an ice cube. If the ice cube melts, it will be a liquid. Water vapor, ice, and liquid water are all the same substance. They are in different states, or phases.

Energy causes the particles of a substance to be in one phase instead of another. Energy causes particles to move faster and farther apart. The phase of a substance can change if you add or take away energy. Putting liquid water in a freezer takes heat energy away. This causes the water to form ice. Putting a pan of water on a lighted burner on a stove adds heat energy. This causes some of the water to form water vapor. Phase changes are examples of physical changes.

frozen water

liquid water

boiling water

The heat from the flame melts the wax part of the candle from a solid into a liquid.

All substances change phases at different temperatures. Ice melts at 0°C, but lead must reach a temperature of 328°C before it will melt. The temperature at which a substance melts is the same temperature at which it freezes.

Other kinds of phase changes are evaporation, or the change from a liquid to a gas, and condensation, or the change from a gas to a liquid. The temperature at which a substance evaporates is the same temperature at which it condenses.

The wax melting in a candle is an example of a phase change. A flame burning above the candle increases the energy in the wax. This causes the solid to melt into a liquid. The liquid will change back to a solid when the wax cools off.

Chemical Changes

Have you ever seen a piece of iron that has rusted? Iron is a shiny, gray metal. Rust is a reddish-brown powdery substance. Iron can form rust when it is left in a damp place. When iron forms rust, a chemical change takes place. A **chemical change** happens when particles of one substance change in some way to form particles of a new substance with different properties. A chemical change produces a new kind of matter.

Heat is often given off during a chemical change. Warm-blooded animals use heat that is given off during chemical changes. Humans use this heat as well. We mix the food we eat with chemicals our bodies have. During this chemical change, heat is given off.

The tarnish that can form on silver is another kind of chemical change. Tarnish is a result of a metal like silver reacting with the air. It causes the silver to turn a dark color.

iron

rusted iron

When wood or paper burns, a chemical change takes place. Both paper and wood are solid substances. When they are lit with a flame, they change from solid substances to ashes, carbon dioxide gas, and water vapor.

vinegar and baking soda

Mixing vinegar and baking soda causes a chemical change. When the acid in vinegar reacts with the baking soda, bubbles of carbon dioxide gas form. The carbon dioxide forces air to go up. The bubbles will rise higher and higher. It almost looks like a volcano erupting!

If you have ever baked bread, you have caused a chemical change. First you mix together ingredients like flour, water, yeast, and salt. Then you bake them in the oven. They have formed a new substance and cannot be changed back to what they were.

When mixed ingredients are baked, a chemical change takes place.

Elements

The particles are alike in a pure substance. Elements are the simplest pure substances. There are more than 100 known elements. Scientists have organized information about these elements in a chart called the periodic table. The row and the column where the element is placed tell something about it. Look at the periodic table on this page and see how many of the elements you may have heard of.

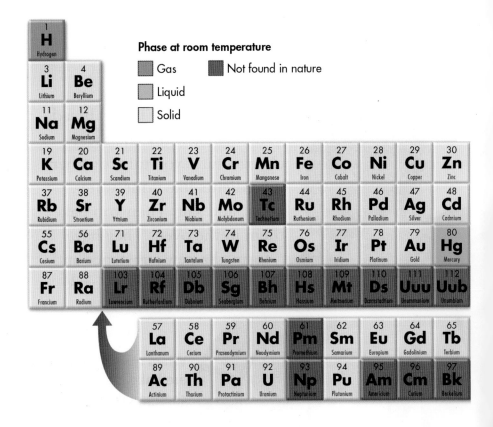

Conclusion

Matter can exist in three forms, or states: solid, liquid, and gas. There are many ways to describe matter. We can use our senses to find out things like how it may look, feel, smell, or taste. We can perform tests to find out about the properties of matter, like the effect of temperature.

You can measure matter to find its mass, volume, or density. Scientists use the metric system to measure matter. Tools such as a balance, a ruler, and a graduated cylinder are used for measuring properties of matter. It is important to use these measuring instruments to compare matter in all its forms.

Matter can change in many ways. It can go through physical and chemical changes. Matter can be found everywhere you look, and it can change at any time.

					2 **He** Helium
5 **B** Boron	6 **C** Carbon	7 **N** Nitrogen	8 **O** Oxygen	9 **F** Fluorine	10 **Ne** Neon
13 **Al** Aluminum	14 **Si** Silicon	15 **P** Phosphorus	16 **S** Sulfur	17 **Cl** Chlorine	18 **Ar** Argon
31 **Ga** Gallium	32 **Ge** Germanium	33 **As** Arsenic	34 **Se** Selenium	35 **Br** Bromine	36 **Kr** Krypton
49 **In** Indium	50 **Sn** Tin	51 **Sb** Antimony	52 **Te** Tellurium	53 **I** Iodine	54 **Xe** Xenon
81 **Tl** Thallium	82 **Pb** Lead	83 **Bi** Bismuth	84 **Po** Polonium	85 **At** Astatine	86 **Rn** Radon

114 **Uuq** Ununquaternium

66 **Dy** Dysprosium	67 **Ho** Holmium	68 **Er** Erbium	69 **Tm** Thulium	70 **Yb** Ytterbium
98 **Cf** Californium	99 **Es** Einsteinium	100 **Fm** Fermium	101 **Md** Mendelevium	102 **No** Nobelium

Glossary

chemical change a change that occurs when particles of one substance change in some way to form particles of a new substance with different properties

density the amount of mass in a certain volume of matter

mixture a blend of two or more substances whose properties do not change when they are combined

physical change any change in the size, shape, or state of matter

solubility a measure of how much of a substance will dissolve in another substance

solute a substance that is dissolved in a solution

solution one or more substances dissolved in another substance

solvent a substance that dissolves another substance